CCSS Genre Folktale

Essential Question
What makes different animals unique?

MW00333983

KING
OF THE BIRDS

A Mayan Folktale

retold by Karen Alexander • illustrated by Linda Bittner

Chapter 1

THE GATHERING

The rain forest was alive with birds. Birds sang in the treetops. They poked among the leaves on the ground, looking for insects to eat. They made nests in the hollows of tree trunks. All day long, the birds also squabbled.

Hawk looked around the forest in dismay. For many years, he had ruled the birds. Now, he was old and tired. Hawk called a meeting of the birds. He told them they must choose a new king who could stop them from fighting.

The birds made plans for a great gathering to choose a king. Each bird secretly thought that it would make the best king.

Mockingbird marched to the front first. She thought she should be king because her voice was more splendid than that of any other bird. To prove her point, she sang her heart out. She sang the songs of other birds. She sang the songs of crickets and frogs.

The other birds were very impressed. They thought that maybe Mockingbird should be king.

Then Cardinal strutted to the front of the meeting. He paraded up and down, showing off his wonderful red feathers. He flapped his wings, and he made the crest, or tuft of feathers, on his head stand up.

The other birds were amazed by Cardinal's beautiful scarlet feathers and his strong beak. They thought that maybe Cardinal would be a good king.

Next, Turkey offered her services as king. She puffed up her chest. Turkey's voice was loud and confident. It reached to the very back of the gathering. Turkey argued her case well. She said that she was big and strong, so she could keep order among the birds. She could stop fights. Turkey said she was also very watchful, so she would be able to keep the birds away from danger.

The other birds listened very carefully. Maybe Turkey should be king.

All day long, birds stepped forward to explain why they should be king. There were birds of all colors and sizes. There were loud birds and quiet birds. There were boastful birds and shy birds. As each bird spoke, the other birds nodded their heads. They whispered among themselves. Maybe this was the bird that should be king.

Only Quetzal kept quiet. The other birds looked at him in disbelief, because Quetzal was known to be proud and ambitious.

Chapter 2
QUETZAL FOR KING!

Now Quetzal had a problem. He knew he was clever and smart. He was sure he was the perfect choice to be king. But his feathers were dull. Then Quetzal thought of Roadrunner—the messenger of the birds. Roadrunner had fabulous, colorful feathers.

Quetzal went into the forest to talk to Roadrunner. He told Roadrunner that she was much too busy to be king. Quetzal boasted about how clever he was. He said that he would make the best king of the birds. The only thing he didn't have was splendid feathers. But Roadrunner did.

Quetzal started to convince Roadrunner to lend Quetzal her feathers. In return, Quetzal promised to share all the riches of being king with his friend.

Now Roadrunner wasn't very happy about this idea. She was fond of her feathers, and, anyway, she would be cold without them. Quetzal was very convincing, though. It wasn't long before he talked Roadrunner into parting with her feathers.

Quetzal didn't give any of his feathers to Roadrunner. He just added Roadrunner's feathers to his own.

A few minutes later, a magnificent bird flew into the meeting, swishing its long, colorful tail. Not only was Quetzal beautiful, but he was also a very strong speaker. In a short time, he had won over all of the birds and he was chosen as the new king.

Chapter 3

ROADRUNNER BETRAYED

Quetzal was very busy being king. He forgot all about his friend Roadrunner.

But, after a few days, the other birds realized they hadn't seen Roadrunner for a while. They searched all through the forest for her.

At last, they found Roadrunner hidden behind a tree. She was cold and hungry. She was hiding because she was too ashamed to be seen in her bare skin.

The birds all helped Roadrunner. They brought food for her, and each bird gave her some of its feathers to keep her warm.

Roadrunner felt warm and well-fed again. However, she was sad because she no longer had her beautiful feathers. Roadrunner's new feathers were many different colors and shapes. She looked odd and patchy. She looked forward to getting her own feathers back.

Roadrunner waited hopefully for Quetzal to bring back her fabulous colorful feathers. But Quetzal didn't ever come back. Even today, Roadrunner races around, anxiously searching the roads for Quetzal.

Summarize

Use details from *King of the Birds* to summarize what was special about each of the different birds. Use your graphic organizer to help you.

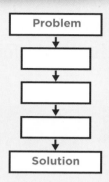

Text Evidence

1. How do you know *King of the Birds* is a folktale? GENRE

2. What problem does Hawk have? What solution does he find? PROBLEM AND SOLUTION

3. Fine the word *squabbled* on page 2. What nearby word helps you figure out what *squabbled* means? SYNONYMS

4. Write about Quetzal's problem and the steps he took to solve the problem. WRITE ABOUT READING

Compare Texts
Read about the unique quetzal.

THE REAL QUETZAL

Quetzals live in Central American rain forests. Male resplendent quetzals have beautiful, bright feathers and a long emerald-green tail. Their bodies are about 15 inches long. Their tails can be twice that long.

Quetzals belong to a family of birds with a unique feature. The two inner toes face backward, and the two outer toes face forward. This helps the birds to perch on the branches of trees. But it makes walking hard, so the birds are not often seen on the forest floor.

Bird Feet	
the foot of most birds	the foot of a quetzal

Resplendent means "dazzling," and these birds have dazzled people for thousands of years. Quetzals were very important in Mayan culture. Their feathers were treasured. The feathers were used to decorate the clothes worn by rulers. They were also traded. The male quetzal's bright green tail feathers were more valuable than gold. For this reason, the birds were seen as a sign of wealth.

Quetzals are heard more often than they are seen. They hide among the green leaves of the forest.

Queztals use their beaks to hollow out a nest in a rotting tree.

Today, quetzals are endangered for two main reasons. First, they are hunted for their feathers. Second, the rain forests where they live are being destroyed. In some countries, the birds are now protected.

Make Connections

How does *The Real Quetzal* help you understand what makes an animal unique? ESSENTIAL QUESTION

How does the description of the quetzal in *The Real Quetzal* help you understand the characteristics of the quetzal mentioned in *King of the Birds*? TEXT TO TEXT

Focus on

Genre

Folktale *King of the Birds* is a folktale. A folktale is a story that is passed down over time by storytellers. Folktales are often very old. This one was told by the Mayans. It could be more than two thousand years old. Each person who tells a folktale changes it a little. Folktales often personify animals as if they have human characteristics. Sometimes they try to teach us a lesson.

Read and Find Many folktales give animals human characteristics, such as greed or vanity. Folktales are not real. The events that occur could not usually happen in real life. For example, in *King of the Birds*, Roadrunner lends her feathers to Quetzal. This could not really happen. Folktales often have a moral. They teach us about human nature and how we should behave.

Your Turn

Write your own folktale. This can be either your version of an old folktale or a new, imaginary folktale. Remember that your story needs to have a message that shows people how to behave.